To. Lynn,
A little help to
one who is confused
hope it helps
Love
James

# CAN WE TALK, LORD?

# CAN WE TALK, LORD?

## PRAYERS FROM A TEENAGER'S HEART

### DAVID GATWARD

First published in 1992 by
KEVIN MAYHEW LTD
Rattlesden
Bury St Edmunds
Suffolk IP30 0SZ

ISBN 086209 223  X

Typesetting & Page Creation by Anne Haskell
Cover Design by Roy Mitchell
Printed in Great Britain by
Fuller-Davies, Ipswich

*To Mum and Dad*
*and my two brothers,*
*John and James.*
*This book is for you.*

# CONTENTS

# ACKNOWLEDGEMENTS

Special Thanks:

**'The Boss'**: Thanks, God! I knew you'd pull it off!

**Dad**: for guiding me all the way (and burning midnight oil because I couldn't type!)

**Mum**: everything I ever needed in a mother (and in such a small package too!)

**John** ('Did you know I play an Ibenez 570 and a Marshall Valvestate?!): for keeping me laughing!*

**James** (THE Horn Player!): the coolest little bro' in the world!

**Stage II**: keep clowning for Christ, guys!

**My Church** (too many people to mention): for your love and support over the years.

**Mustard Seed and specially Kate**: for showing me 'The Man' so that instead of just 'sitting there' I decided to 'stand up and be counted'.

**Dave** (No. 2 of the 'Dynamic Duo'): for being there at the beginning (remember Rocketown).

**Sarah** (Screwball!): the nearest thing I'll ever have to a sister.

**The TFG Gang**: hey, guys! I did it!

**Emma**: for discovering my prayers and persuading her dad to publish them.

*Love ya, Bro!

# FOREWORD

When told this book was to be published, I
couldn't believe it! 'Me? My own book?', I
thought. 'Impossible!' Well, obviously not,
because here it is! The reason I was so
surprised was because I really didn't think
that the prayers were anything special, just
conversations between myself and The Boss.
I'd written them down as an aid to my own
prayer, basically to get rid of the 'ems' and
'ers' that so often appeared! But I guess The
Boss had other ideas! (Doesn't he always!)

I really only started writing them at the
end of my first year at sixth form college. I
was at the 'Spaghetti Junction' in my life and
I felt so mangled and confused inside that
one night, at a drama presentation by some
friends, during a song called 'How can you
sit there?', it all became too much and I just
put my head in my hands and cried, and
cried, and cried. The pressure was just too
much and at that point I realised what was
missing. I'd been a Christian for as long as I
could remember, but I'd wandered away,
becoming more and more preoccupied with
'other' things. Now I realised I needed Jesus,
and when the call to go forward came,
myself and a close friend walked to the front,
tears streaming down our faces to the warm
embraces of our friends. And I'll never forget

the words of the minister that night. As I got up on the stage he looked at me and said, 'God loves you, Dave. Welcome home!' Then he hugged me as I cried on his shoulder. But what a thought! 'Welcome home!' Jesus had welcomed me home and accepted me as I was – mangled, rotten, fed up and confused. I was home.

Now I'm not saying that was the answer; in fact things got a whole lot worse during the next year but, with Jesus, I was able to pull through – I still remember the nights I cried myself to sleep, punching the pillow and yelling 'Why? Why me, Lord?' But he stuck by me.

So there you go! That's how this book happened. Nothing special, just prayers from a teenager. All I hope is that they help you to realise Jesus isn't a long way away but is in fact very close. He's the best friend you'll ever have, and he loves a good chat. So how about it?

God Bless,

P.S. Some of the prayers have my name, age, etc., included in them. To make them more personal *please* change them to suit you when praying to the The Boss! Hope they help!

## MY FAMILY

Lord, you there?
It's about my family.
I've been thinking about them
    for a while now.
What is it?
Why is it?
Who is it?

First, there's my 'real' family.
Mum,
Dad,
    two brothers,
    and a mixed bag of relatives!
Lord, I love them all!
Thanks for my family;
    they're the best,
    they've helped me so much.
We've had our problems,
    our arguments.
But the tears always gave way to smiles,
    and laughter,
    and happiness.
Thanks, Lord!

And then, there's my wider family,
    those 'out there'.
Not just the Church, Lord,

though I am grateful for it,
for the Christian family,
my friends back at church,
and in the youth group.
But it's the wider family that's
on my mind,
the ones really 'out there'.
For they too are my brothers, and sisters,
and your children.
The homeless,
the hungry,
the poverty stricken,
and the terminally ill.
The Aids sufferers,
the disadvantaged,
the junkies,
and those who, for whatever reason,
are locked away.
The list is endless, Lord.
So many unhappy people,
and so many of them who
don't know you.

And all of them are my brothers,
my sisters, your children.
It hurts, Lord.
It hurts to see my family in such a mess,

to see it spoiled,
so torn apart by hate,
misunderstanding,
a lack of trust,
a famine of love.

Lord,
Father,
I thank you for what I have.
Please forgive me for so often
forgetting how fortunate I am,
and for ignoring those who do
not have  what I have.
Those with no family, no friends,
no love, no you!

Help my brothers and sisters, Lord,
your children.

Amen.

## LORD, CAN WE TALK?

Lord, can we talk?
I feel daft praying about this again
    but I feel I've got no one else to talk to –
    just you.
It's girls again!
That time-old problem.
What am I going to do, Lord?
I'm so confused.
It's so painful knowing what I could do
    if I were home.
But I'm not !
I'm here,
    a hundred miles away from
    a very special person.
It's not fair, God!
Remember her letter?
And how about when we said
    'goodbye'?
'Go and find someone good enough
    for you', she said.
For goodness sake – I was saying
    goodbye to her!
The person good enough for me;
    now gone!
She hasn't even written.
Can't blame her really.

After my last letter,
    and knowing now how I feel.
My God. Why?
Come on, Lord, would you write?
I gave her no choice I guess.
Went out on my own before
    consulting you.
But I love her! (At least I think I do!)
What I'd do given half the chance.
If only I knew how to make her love me.
But I don't.
And even if I did, no use it'd be,
    being here.
I'm a victim of geography.
I've lost again, God,
    I've lost again!
And I don't know what to do;
    I daren't write,
    I daren't 'phone.
I'm so screwed up.
What chance is there for anything
    with a hundred mile gap?
All through the others
I knew deep down how I really felt,
    yet I had to spend two years,
    helping her through!
Holding myself back from reaching out.

Lord, you know how I really fell for her.
Good grief, even mum and dad
    could tell!
'Hang in there', I get told.
'It depends how much you want her.'
But, Lord, all I can do is sit and cry!
Cry about a  friendship.
One that became the centre of my life,
    one I so wanted to develop into
    something more.
It was never given a chance.
But even though I 'may' have
    lost a girlfriend
    (and the 'may' is in your hands,
    Lord!),
    I gained the greatest, most caring,
    understanding, and lovely
    person as a friend.
Thank you, Lord.

Amen.

# LORD, I'VE A FEW QUESTIONS

Lord, you got a minute?
It's just that I've a few questions – again!
This week's been quite good,
    Lord, really.
    (Not 'boring' as I'd expected!)
Making friends, learning, talking.
Great stuff.
But there's this problem.
I may be paranoid,
    but it seems to me that everyone
    else has more to offer than I do!
Those with the 'rock-solid' faith.
The ones who know the Bible
    from cover to cover.
Those who don't mind saying
    what they think.
And me?
Well exactly . . . me?!
Come on, Lord, are you crazy?
I'm a clown, a long-haired idiot!
My faith has so many holes in it
    you could use it as a sieve!
I lose my temper,
    get angry if someone disagrees with me.
And to be honest, Lord, I find
    the Bible quite boring.
So what on earth *can* I offer?

Maybe I'm not the only one
   who feels like the worst
   christian in the world.
Look at Peter.
He was a hot-headed fisherman
   with a tendency to speak first,
   and think later.
He even denied you three times.
Yet look what you did with him!

But that's you isn't it, Lord?
You like ordinary people.
You were a carpenter,
   your disciples,
   fishermen, tax collectors,
   and now me!!
And for that, Lord, I thank you.
Thank you for choosing me,
   and for accepting me as I am.

Amen.

# LORD, ARE YOU THERE?

Lord, are you there?
It's just that I'm on my own
     and I need someone to talk to.
     (You don't mind if we have a chat,
     do you, Lord?)
I've just moved out, left home.
It's kind of strange really.
You can't go downstairs
     and expect someone to be there,
     watching TV
     and ready for a chat.
There's no vast pool of friends to call on.
The church is strange.
People are strange.
You're suddenly on your own.
You say to yourself, 'it'll be fine'.
Convince yourself nothing
     can shake you.
Tell your family,
     'Don't worry, I'll be OK.'
I'm not saying I'm depressed, Lord,
     or totally friendless or lonely.
It's just that it's a bit of a shock
     to the system.
It's so weird being away from home.
I keep running the fact I've left home
     over and over in my mind.

How did you feel when you left
  home, Lord?

Did you feel lonely?

Lord, this brings up the thought
  of your call to us.
You said we have to leave our families
  and take up our cross and follow you.
Do you know how hard that is, Lord?
My family mean so much to me.
They've helped me so much.
And my friends have too.
Some of them are so very special.
I can't cope if I lose touch with them.
My social life,
  my hobbies,
  my life.
Lord, don't you think it's too
  much to ask?
To give up everything for you?
How can I, Lord?
How?

'David, listen to me!
I gave up everything.
I was rejected in my home town.
I was betrayed by one of

my closest friends.
I was denied three times.
They couldn't even stay awake for me.
And then I died, David.
I died for you.
I died so that you could know me.
I will never leave you, David.
I will always be by your side.
Because I love you
I ask you to follow me.'

Amen.

# DREAMS

Life depends on dreams;
    the ambitions of the heart,
    that private yearning
    for something special.

Yet once caught
    they are like china in your hand,
    beautiful but fragile,
    and easily broken.

But if we shy away from our dreams,
    afraid of losing something
    we so cherished,
    we will never realise the beauty
    of something that was truly
    and uniquely ours,
    no matter how short lived.

A life of dreams is better than
    a life of regrets.
Grasp them while you can
    and hold them tight,
    for tomorrow they may be gone.

Amen.

# CONFUSED

You got a minute, Lord?
It's about being, well, er, kind
   of confused.
Everything and nothing is happening
   at the same time!
Decisions to be made.
Work to be done.
Problems to be solved.
Do you understand, Lord?
It's not so much a case of being lost,
   more of a 'spaghetti junction' in life.
Where do I go, Lord?
Where are the signposts?
Which road do I follow?
I've so much I want to do,
   yet so little I can.

Are my thoughts clouded, Lord?
Sometimes I despair.
It just doesn't seem worth it.
I want to run, Lord, get away.
From you, friends, work, life.
Everything.
Is it worth carrying on, Lord?
I see no light at the end of the tunnel.
Where are you in this swirling darkness?
Are you testing me, Lord?

It's at times like these
    that I need you most,
Yet . . . I get no answer.

I don't want to be rude, Lord, but . . .
    do you really exist?
It seems that logically you don't exist,
    yet at the same time you do!
You know what I mean, Lord?
Do you really understand?
Are you confused?
I really wonder sometimes, Lord,
    whether,
    well you know, what if?
Perhaps . . .
Why?
If only!!
CONFUSED!!

Oh, Lord, help me to untangle
    the lines of my thoughts.
To see your purpose for me ahead.
I don't want to be confused
    anymore, Lord.
It's confusing!!

Amen.

# ALONE

Lord, can't you hear me?
Don't you hear my cry of pain?
Are you there, in the darkness?
Don't you know the way I feel?

DAVID, I AM HERE!

Lord, I am lost, can't you find me?
I'm knocking, Lord,
    why won't you answer?
I'm alone, Lord,
    why won't you comfort me?
I'm hurt, why won't you heal?

DAVID, I AM HERE!

Lord, I don't know which way to turn.
I'm alone, lost, and confused.
The love I seek is gone.
Where are you, Lord?

DAVID, I AM HERE!

Help me, Lord!
The darkness it surrounds me!
I scrabble in the dust, alone on my knees.
My heart has been pierced,

and my love rejected.
My life seems in ruins.
Won't you help me?

DAVID, I AM HERE!

My hand is outstretched for you!
I love you and will never leave you!
Why won't you listen?
Why won't you trust?
How weak your faith is!

I AM HERE!

Lord??
Is that you??

Amen.

# PRAYER

Lord, it's about prayer.
Well, it's just I don't know how to . . .
     well, you know,
     pray.
What is it, Lord?
How do you start?
What do you pray about?
Who do you pray to?
     God?
     Jesus?
     Father?
     Mother?
     Lord?
     Dad?!!
It's not easy, you know.
There's never been any real guide
     to follow.
'101 Ways to Pray!!'
Not a bad idea really is it?
It's all very well this Christian stuff,
     but how do you go about it?
Can't you give us even a tiny hint?
You say we should listen.
How do we do that when our minds
     are so full up we just forget to pray?
Never mind listen!
How do we know if you've heard us?

How do we know if we've
    been answered?
Do you understand, Lord?
It isn't just me is it?
I often wonder if I'm the only Christian
    doing everything the wrong way!!
But is there a wrong way, Lord?
Is there any way?

Bear with me, Lord.
It's tough but please keep helping me.
Even though I find it all so hard
    I know I'd be lost without you.
You know what I really mean,
    even if my prayers don't say it.
You know what I need,
    not what I think I need.
Help me to trust your decision, Lord,
    even though it might hurt.
Pick me up when I fall down.
Heal my broken faith
    when I begin to doubt.
Teach me to pray, Lord.
Please!!

Amen.

# PARENTS

Hi, Lord, got a minute?
Well, it's about parents.
What are they, Lord?
One minute you hate 'em,
    next you love 'em!
'I've been there too,' they say.
Have they?
Are you sure they're not made in
    a 'parent factory'?
A production line, each given the
    necessary items for parenthood.
Yet, if that's so, why do they seem so
    incompetent when it comes to us,
    the *adolescents*?
Are we that hard to understand, Lord?
Surely parents are there to help.
Then why do they always seem
    to hinder,
    never understand,
    jump to conclusions,
    and treat you like a child?
I thought they'd 'been there'!


Do you know what I mean, Lord?
They shout and scream at you, saying:
    'I wonder if it's worth it.' or,

'I wouldn't have got away with that
when I was your age!'

Teach them to listen, Lord.
To understand.
We know we're not perfect,
    but a little love and
    encouragement go a long way.
We know they love us, Lord,
    we really do.
Without them we'd never pull through.
Just let them know, Lord, how we feel.
And that although we find life difficult,
    we still love them,
    and always will.

Amen.

## GROWING UP

Lord, I'm alone,
    alone in my room.
Shut off from the turmoil of
    the outside world.
The only sound the soft, calculated
    ticking of my clock.
It gives me time, Lord, to gather
    my thoughts.
The problems of teenage life;
    adolescence.
It's strange, Lord, being 17.
Not an adult and not a child.
Yet expected to be one or the other
    several times a day.
Have adults forgotten that they were
    teenagers once?
Surely they should be filled with advice
    and help?
Yet all they do is shout and tell you
    to 'grow up'.
What is 'growing up', Lord?
If it means becoming like them, Lord,
    I don't want to.
They've stopped growing, Lord.
They think they've arrived.
No more to learn.
I don't want to be like that, Lord.

I want to be 'growing up'
    not a 'grown up'.
I never want to stop learning.
I want to remember what it's like
    being a teenager,
      and be able to understand how they feel.
I don't want to forget,
    like so many of the grown-ups today.

Why don't they understand, Lord?
Do we frighten them?
Are they scared of us?
We only want to be heard, Lord,
    understood . . .
    loved . . .

Don't they realise that, Lord?
Are they blind?

I don't think it's us that need help,
    Lord – it's them.

Amen.

# I WANT

Lord, I just want to apologise.
I'm sorry for wanting.
Everytime I pray, it's all 'I want'.
And the things I want are usually
    so trivial,
    unimportant,
    unnecessary.

This time I want –
    to stop wanting!
I want to stop asking.
Prayer's supposed to be more
    than a list of requests
    that leave me angry
    when I don't get what I ask for.
What am I doing, Lord?
For not only am I upset
    when I don't get what I want,
    but then I forget to say
    thanks when I do!
Why do you bother?
You must get sick of being
    unappreciated.
I'm sorry.

Lord, help me to stop asking,
    to stop wanting,

to just trust.
If I 'need' something,
    as long as you think I do
    then I know I'll get it.
And, Lord, if I don't,
    help me to understand why;
    why you said, 'No'.

And finally, Lord,
    help me to be what you want me to be.
And not what I want to be.

Amen.

# CHRISTMAS!

On the first day of Christmas
    my true love sent to me
    four bars of chocolate,
    a large turkey,
    three Christmas puddings,
    and a huge iced Christmas cake!

On the second day of Christmas
    I saw a picture from Ethiopia
    of a family starving in the hot desert.
Their tired legs worn out
    after many miles of walking
    in search of food.
Yet still their bowls are empty.

On the third day of Christmas
    my true love sent to me
    a new television,
    and a radio-cassette player.

On the fourth day of Christmas
    I turned on my television
    and saw a picture of a polluted river,
    its swirling mass carrying before it
    the decaying matter from everything
    it had touched.

The fish, birds, and plants
that were once so attractive
now gone forever.

On the fifth day of Christmas
my true love sent to me
a chain made of gold,
and a ring of silver.

On the sixth day of Christmas
I walked past a queue
outside the Job Centre.
So many people wanting to work,
to earn some money,
when no jobs are available.

On the seventh day of Christmas
my true love sent to me
a card wishing 'good health,
and cheer for the New Year'.

On the eighth day of Christmas
I walked past a young girl on the streets
wrapped in a sleeping bag
and huddled inside a brown
cardboard box.

On the ninth day of Christmas
    my true love sent to me
    a song she had written,
    expressing her love for me.

On the tenth day of Christmas
    two young children walked by
    me in the street;
    no shoes on their feet,
    their clothes tattered and torn.
Who was giving them the love
    they needed?

On the eleventh day of Christmas
    my true love sent to me
    a picture of the baby Jesus
    in the stable with Mary and Joseph
    looking adoringly at him.

On the twelfth day of Christmas . . .
    I sat down and cried.
    I cried for all who went without
    this year.
No love,
    no warmth,
    no home,

no family,
no food.

Why am I celebrating Christmas?

And then I remembered . . .
    a cross,
    and an empty tomb.
I remembered a baby coming
    as Light into a world
    of cold uncaring darkness.
A child of hope and peace,
    a child of salvation.
The Son of God,
    born for me,
    born for all!
A child to become the man
    who could change all things
    and all people!

Amen.

# MEMORIES

Lord, can you remember
    my first attempt at riding a bike?
Yes, I know! I rode into a wall!
A long time ago that, Lord,
    a long time ago.
Memories . . . ah, what strange things.
Happy times,
    sad times,
        some just forgotten.
It's strange looking back.
I can sit for hours just remembering,
    looking through old photos,
    newspaper cuttings.
The occasional tear trickling
    down my cheek.

Looking back, Lord, my life
    has been pretty great so far.
I've done so much already.
There are periods I can remember
    which were tough;
        sitting there wondering why
        everything was going wrong.
Yet those times, Lord, I now realise
    were necessary,
        each one allowing me to develop
        in a different way,

to grow up a little,
and learn a bit more.
Then there are the happy times.
Lord, I can never thank you enough
for the happiness that has filled my life.
Just thinking about it makes me smile,
and even laugh at some
of the things I did.


You know, Lord, I think I can almost see
a faint smile appear on your face!
A warm, happy, reminiscing smile.
You can remember too can't you, Lord?
Do you remember those days in Galilee?
Sunny days, down by the lake?
Childhood days in Nazareth?
I'd give anything to know about
that part of your life.
Did you get into trouble?
Did you get told off?
And, if you don't mind me asking, Lord,
did you have girl trouble?
Yes, Lord, I knew I could see a smile.
You can remember!
Happy times, and sad times.
That life so long ago.

Did you ever think you'd have
    such an effect?
Can you still remember your
    death, Lord?
When the nails tore through
    your wrists
    when they hung you up,
    and you looked down
    on your mother,
    knowing you were going to die.
Do you remember it, Lord?
Do you?

'Yes, David, I remember.
I remember the pain,
    the crown of thorns,
    the thought of dying.
I even remember the feeling
    of the burning sun upon my back,
    and the look on my mother's face
    as I hung there.
Yes, David, I remember it.
I can remember every bead of sweat,
    every ounce of pain,
    every drop of blood,
    from that terrible day.

My hands still clench
    as I remember the nails.

But, David, I also remember why I died,
    why I suffered.
I died for you, David.
Remember?

Amen.

## BOY MEETS GIRL

Lord, are you there?
Have you got time for a chat?
Well, I just need to talk;
  talk about a problem.
It's not just mine though.
I guess all teenagers (and adults!)
  find it hard;
  the dreaded first date,
  the first kiss . . .
Lord, why is it so hard?
And not just the first time,
  but every time?
How do you approach them?
How do you let them know
  you're interested
  without coming on too strong?
How do you know
  if they're interested in you?
And why does it seem easier
  for everyone other than me?!
Good grief, Lord, take it from me,
  this boy/girl stuff is agony!
One minute you're in love,
  next minute you hate each other!
Then, you just about get it together,
  and suddenly you've left home,
  and there's no chance!

Isn't it strange
    how this person seems to be
    the one for you,
    without whom you'd die
    of a broken heart,
    unable to go on!
Couldn't you make it easier, Lord?
You know, actually TELL us if it is
    the right one,
    or if we actually stand a chance?
It's all so hit and miss.
    (I'm not the only one who feels
    like this, am I, Lord?)

I know I'm asking a bit too much,
    and I'm sorry.
If I'm honest I have to admit
    that even though a lot of pain
    and heartache is involved,
    it's still exciting!
In fact a lot of it is good fun!
When it does work out,
    even for a short time,
    it's fantastic!

Lord, thank you for giving me
    the ability to survive

the turmoils of teenage love.
Give me the courage and strength
    to keep going.
Help me to get better at this
    'game of love'.
Finally, Lord, I pray that when I do find
    'the one',
        you will be there to keep us together,
        and to help it last.

Amen.

# WHERE AM I?

Lord, remember when I was five?
When I got lost in the supermarket?
I wanted mum and dad,
    wanted to go home.
Like now.
I'm not in a supermarket though,
    I'm just lost.
Where am I?
Where do I go?
What do I do?

Why is life so confusing?
Why do I keep getting lost?

Are you there, Lord?
Sometimes I even lose you,
    or that's the way it seems.
I wander off on my own.
I 'know the way',
    or that's what I imagine,
    and I forget to ask you,
    'Where do I go?
    Which way do I take?'

Lord, help me to stop getting lost,
    and help me to find my way home,
    to you.

Amen.

# HONESTY

Lord, it's about being honest . . .
    and, to be honest,
    I don't know where to start.
Honesty can be good, and bad.
It can get you into trouble,
    lose you friends,
    leave you standing on your own.
For example, Lord,
    say I didn't like someone . . .
    does that mean I tell them?
That's being honest isn't it?
What if I see a tramp steal a hamburger
    because he'd had nothing to eat
    for a couple of days . . .
    do I turn him over?

You know, Lord,
I think a few guidelines on this
    would have been useful.
When to be honest.
How to be honest.
Being honest to yourself.
The pros and cons of honesty.
Ever considered it?


Do I sound a bit confused, Lord?

I'm not really. . . well, not much.
I think my real problem is about
    being honest with myself.
I'm not the wonderful guy I like
    to think I am.
I'm not full of confidence,
    and I'm definitely not
    happy all the time.
In fact, Lord, I don't even consider
    myself to be a good
    example of Christianity.
I look at myself and often don't
    like what I see.
I'm not good enough to be
    associated with you, Lord.
To be honest, I find it hard to
    understand why you love me.

But, Lord, that's why I
    keep coming back.
Being honest with myself
    is admitting I can't survive
    without you.
I need you every hour of every day.
Please stay with me, Lord.
I need you, I honestly do!

Amen.

## SAYING SORRY

Lord, you there?
I need a bit of help.
It's about saying sorry.
In the words of Elton John:
    'Sorry seems to be the hardest word'.
Why is it, Lord?
It's easy enough to pronounce,
    easy to spell,
    takes very little energy to say.
So, where's the problem?

It's not the saying it that's the
    problem though, is it, Lord?
It's the reason for saying it.
The accepting that you're wrong,
    the fact that you have to
    admit to someone
    that you have to say
    sorry to them.
It hits home, Lord,
    damages your self-image,
    your pride, your confidence,
    your credibility.

And therein lies the problem – PRIDE.
Too proud to say 'sorry'.
I wonder how many friendships
    have been spoilt

because someone was too
proud to say, 'I'm sorry'.
Just how many marriages would
still be going
if only one partner had turned
and said, 'I'm sorry'?

'I'm sorry.'
Surely it doesn't hurt that much?

Teach me to say, 'sorry', Lord.
To admit when I'm wrong
and have the courage to admit it,
even if it does hurt.
To achieve that could save
a friendship, a marriage, a life.

And, Lord, teach me to forgive,
to hold no grudges even when
those concerned don't say 'sorry'.

Forgive me, Lord, for not saying 'sorry'
and for not offering forgiveness.
I am sorry.


Amen.

# HA! HA! HA!

Lord, what do you call a cat that's
    eaten a duck?
A duck-filled fatty puss!
Ha! Ha! Ha!
Yes, Lord, I love laughter.
It's definitely one of the greatest gifts
    you've given us.
There's nothing better than a good
    rib-tickling, side-aching,
    eye-crying, laugh!
Laughter can be the best medicine.
You can feel down, upset,
    ill, depressed, alone,
    tired – anything.
But just a small laugh, a quiet giggle,
    and it's all different.
You actually feel better!
Kind of warm inside.
Yep, humour is God-given.
And you, Lord,
    I think you've got quite a
    sense of humour too.
In fact, I can picture you on the
    shore of Lake Galilee,
    sitting around a small fire, cooking fish,
    drinking, and laughing!
Yes, Lord, laughing!

Laughing with Peter, and John,
    laughing with your disciples,
    telling jokes, chuckling with each
    other, pulling each other's leg.
Yes, Lord, you laughed!

And you know,
    I can see your sense of humour
    in the world you made.
Take people.
Boy, are there some funny people!
They walk funny, talk funny, dress funny.
Just take a walk down a city street,
    and it's hard not to burst out laughing!

And then there's nature.
Some of your creations are truly
    wonderful and hilarious!
Just watching puppies play,
    lambs running round a field,
    a squirrel eating a hazel nut.
Each one brings a smile.

Yes, Lord, your sense of humour!
What a gift!
Thanks for laughter, Lord, it's hilarious!
Amen.

## ALL LIES

Lord, you there?
Just a word, if you're not busy.
It's just that something's come up.
I didn't expect it. Not surprising really.

A friend called just now, just to say, 'Hi'.
An innocent face bringing bad news.
Without realising they told me,
told me what another 'friend' had done.

I stood there, Lord, kind of stunned.
'My friend lied to me?' I thought.
OK, some people lie without meaning to,
    small, 'unthought-about' lies.
But this, Lord, was carefully thought
    out, planned.

Why not come out with the truth?
Why the need to hide behind a lie?
It hurt, Lord; it really hurt.

My friend, Lord,
    whom I remember with affection.
The times we shared, the laughter,
    the happiness, the sadness, the trust.
What now, dear friend?
Why the change of face?
Why turn your back?

Don't you remember me?
Do you really hate me?
Why did you lie?

Lord, you still there?
I suppose, Lord, looking at it,
    the hurt I feel is because of
    all the guilt.
The fact that I've really been the cause
    of all this.
My fault.

Unwittingly sowing the seeds.
Those few words said in anger.
The talking behind the back.
Yet I knew then, Lord,
    what would happen. I knew.
I saw from the very beginning.

And now, Lord, I come back,
    back to you, my true friend.
The friend who loves
    and forgives me no matter what I do.
Help me to understand
    and forgive my friend, Lord,
    so that I may, if only in a small way,
    be like you.

Amen.

## SEX!!

Lord, can we talk?
It's about SEX.
The three-letter word,
    abused by some,
    loved by others,
    the subject of jokes,
    the cause of giggling in
    a class of eleven year olds,
    even the cause of embarrassment.
All due to one word.

What is it about that small word
    that scares people?
It brings them out in a cold sweat!
They stutter, go red.
All due to that one word.
To be honest, Lord, so do I.
The trouble is, is that, well, er . . .
    actually, Lord, what is the trouble?
Everyone is either male or female,
    their sex.
To produce offspring,
    all species have sex.
Couples use sex as a way of expressing
    their love for one another.

There, all wrapped up, neat and tidy.
But it's not that easy, Lord, is it?

Sex is a problem.
First, and most important for me,
   is the 'pre-marital sex' problem.
Lord, I really understand why people
   sleep with each other.
When the lights are low, the music soft,
   the two of you are on your own,
   it's hard to say 'no'.

So many people do it.
So many of my friends do it.
It seems to be a part of life,
   completely natural.
But if only they knew.
Lord, sex is a gift from you.
And it's not given for the cheap thrill.

Lord, I'd be a liar if I said I'd never
   wanted to sleep with someone.
Of course I have.
Everyone has or will do.
We're only human.
The sexual urge is natural, normal.
It's controlling it that's the problem!
If only people were more open,
   more willing to understand.
Many my age think,
'Well, I've done it now, so why stop?'

There's only one reason, Lord:
    I want to save myself for
    that one special person.
I don't want to be there, and say,
    'You're the twentieth person
    I've slept with'.
I want to give that person all of me.
But that's me, Lord.
Where does that leave those that have
    slept around a bit,
    those that feel it's too late?
They've spoilt something precious,
    and irreplaceable,
    and now can't be forgiven?
Please, Lord, tell them.
Tell them they're not alone,
    that you understand,
    and that they are forgiven.

Help us all, Lord, to come to
    terms with sex.
Not to shy away from it, not to give in.
But to realise how important
    and beautiful it is.
To remember how fragile it is.
Never to forget it is your gift to us.
Amen.

# NOT AGAIN!

Lord, it's happened again!
Another Grade E and I worked so hard,
    (at least, I think I did).
I did all the research, asked dad about it,
    even mentioned it to you,
    so what went wrong?
Why an E?
I really thought I'd done well.
'I'll show them', I thought.
But I was wrong, just another bad grade.
Why is everyone else in the class
    better than me?
Am I thick? And what's really annoying
    is that they don't even bother about
    you, and yet they still do well!
Why? It's not fair!
Come on, Lord, I know I'm asking
    for something again,
    but please help me to make
    the next one a bit better.
I want to show them,
    show them that I can do it . . .
    show them that I'm not thick!
And, Lord, if it is another E
    help me to keep trying,
    and not give up.
(Could I have a D next time, Lord, please . . .)
Amen.

# THANKS, LORD

Lord, thank you!
I just felt I had to say it!
So many times I've come to you,
 shouting,
 screaming,
 yelling.
Telling you you're wrong!
Arguing with you!
Only bothered about myself,
 and how I'm feeling.
Well this time, Lord,
 I just want to say, thanks.
Thanks for everything.

For my family, Lord;
 I do love them.
They've stuck by me,
 brought me up.
I love them, Lord, thanks!

My friends.
Where would I be without them?
OK, we have our arguments,
 but they keep me going,
 talk to me, laugh with me,
 (and at me!)
They make me happy.
Thanks for them, Lord.

Oh, and thanks for music.
I'd go mad without it!
From the hard loud, rock
    to the soft and thoughtful classical,
    each expressing a different mood,
    be it the desire to jump and dance,
    or the wanting to sit and cry.
Music helps me get through each day,
    express feelings that otherwise
    remain silent.
Music! I love it!

Thanks also, Lord, for the countryside,
    and its beauty.
From the valley to the field,
    the river to the stream,
    the awesome mountains
    to the soft rolling hills.
Thanks for the wildlife
    that makes it come alive;
    the foxes, rabbits,
    birds, insects.
All of it, Lord, pointing to your
    creative genius.
Such fantastic artwork!
Thanks, Lord!
And thanks also for people.

So much potential, in that which
    is small and vulnerable!
We have the ability to think and learn,
    to create,
    (and sadly, to destroy),
    to love, laugh,
    cry, hear, see.
Lord, I feel I could go on forever,
    the list seems endless!

So much to say thank you for:
    family,
    friends,
    music,
    life,
    countryside,
    love,
    home,
    church,
    wildlife,
    food,
    happiness,
    adventure,
    excitement,
    sport,
    clothes . . .
Lord, I could just keep on going!

But there is just one more thing to add.
Thank you, Lord, for loving me!

Amen.

# LOVE

Lord, it's about 'love'.
That word, that wonderful
    four letter word.
Did you ever realise that it would
    hold  so much power?
Have so many meanings?
Can we just think about it
    for a moment, Lord?
Because I have to admit
    that I find it all rather confusing.

LOVE
What is it, Lord?
What does it mean?
For it's used in so many different ways,
    each one almost contradicting
    the others.
How many people say 'I love'
    without realising the full
    potential of that word?
For example, Lord,
    I love chocolate,
    and I also love music,
    and going to the theatre.
Yet at the same time
    I also love my family,
    I love my friends,
    I love you!

You see?
I use the same word but to mean
    something different each time!
I can hardly compare my
    love of chocolate
    with the love I have for my family!

And then also, Lord, I can think
    of other situations:
    when, 'I love you' is whispered
    into a loved one's ear,
    or you 'make love' with your partner.
(Now there's an interesting
    thought, Lord!)
How do you make love?
Are there special ingredients?
'Leave for 1-2 hours in the oven,
    until brown on top'!

Quite humorous don't you think, Lord?
But maybe not so far from the truth.
You know, Lord,
    I think there are special
    ingredients that make for real love.

Remember that passage from
    the Bible, Lord?

*Love is very patient and kind,*
*never jealous or envious,*
*never boastful or proud,*
*never haughty or selfish or rude.*
*Love does not demand its own way.*
*It is not irritable or touchy.*
*It does not hold grudges,*
*and will hardly even notice*
*when others do it wrong.*
*It is never glad about injustice,*
*but rejoices whenever truth wins out.*
*If you love someone*
*you will be loyal to them*
*no matter what the cost.*
*You will always believe in them,*
*always expect the best of them.*
*And always stand your ground*
*in defending them.'*

I Corinthians 13:4 - 7

The ingredients of love.
A long recipe for such a small word!

But just as a final request, Lord,
    teach me to love.
To love the way you love

each and every one of us,
no matter what we do.
And above all, Lord,
    help me to love you.

Amen.

# FRIENDSHIP

Lord, you there?
I just want to have a chat for a minute.
It's not really a 'thank you' prayer
    or a 'questioning' prayer,
    not even an 'angry'
    or 'confused' prayer.
Just a chat.

It's about friendship.
A single word that means so much.
First, Lord, I guess I should say thanks.
You've made my life so full
    of friends and friendship.
Some I've lost contact with,
    some I've drifted away from.
Others I've lost through argument,
    and some were nothing but
    candles in the wind.
But without each of them my life
    would have been poorer.
Together they've given the happiness,
    guidance, and love that I've needed.
And for that I thank you
    and remember each one before you,
    by each individual name.

Yep, friends are pretty great!

But, Lord, we both know the problems,
    don't we?
How some imagine that friendship
    is easy:
    no problems,
    easy come, easy go.

Not so, Lord!
I've learnt from experience,
    how hard and demanding
    friendships can be.
For each of us is different.
It's not that I'm complaining,
    just recognising that those differences
    often become barriers.
Everyone is going to come across people
    they don't get on with.
The dreaded 'personality clash'!
Believe me, Lord,
    I've met a few that I just can't stand!
Their habits irritate,
    their talk jars (and never stops!)
They get on my nerves,
    discredit what I say,
    and laugh at what I believe.
Lord, there are some people
    I just don't like!

Mind you, I guess ~~guess~~ I'm as much
 to blame.
I'm stubborn, big headed,
 loud-mouthed, short tempered,
 always think I'm right
 and have the answer.
I'm surpirised anyone gets on
 at all with me!
But then there are others,
 those I can and do get on with.
They have the same sense of humour,
 similar interests,
 and ideas and beliefs.
I enjoy their company,
 and we become friends.
I guess I have many friends like that,
 'buddies', 'mates',
 call them what you want.
The ones you see at school,
 meet at youth club.
Friendships you enjoy,
 but that you sadly drift in and
 out of for no other reason
 than you're growing up.

But as you do,
 so the friendship of one or two

becomes more important.
You talk more,
    learn more about each other,
    and discover the meaning of trust.
And if the friendship becomes
    really special,
    so you come to love each other.
Friends like this, I really thank you for.
Without them, their care and support,
    I'd be lost.
You can have arguments, and fall out,
    but for what has been gained and shared,
    I thank you, Lord.
For each one has taught me just a little
    more about life,
    about people,
    the world,
    and you.
For you are my greatest friend.

Lord, I thank you for friendship,
    and I pray that you will help me,
    not only to appreciate my friends,
    but to be a friend.


Amen.

# BOREDOM

Lord,
I'm bored!
Dead bored!
Totally bored!
Completely and utterly bored!

B - O - R - E - D!

Bored.
Nothing to do.
No one to talk to.
Nowhere to go.
Totally bored.
So I thought we might have a chat.
I hope you don't mind.

Do you get bored, Lord?
Have times when you've nothing to do?
Just sitting around, kicking your heels,
    doodling on a heavenly bit of paper?

What is boredom, Lord?
Does it really exist?
And if so, why?
There's no reason for it,
    it's just there.
Just look at this world.

So much to see, so much to do.
When I think about it there's no reason
    to be bored.
In fact I don't think boredom exists!
But *laziness* does!!

Laziness, the 'can't be bothered' attitude.
Not bored, just lazy.
Why are we lazy?
Again I can't see any reason for it,
    none at all.
There's so much to do,
    so much needing to be done.
So why is it we can't be bothered?

Lord, save me from my laziness.
Help me not to become bored,
    and forgive me for the excuses I make
    for my laziness, and my boredom.
Show me that there is so much
    to see and do,
    and so little time to achieve any of it.

Lord, stop me from being bored.
It's so boring!!

Amen.

# EXAMS

AAAARRRRGGGGHHHH!
Lord!
I HATE EXAMS!
GCSE! A Levels!
Exams!
No matter how small or large,
    important or insignificant,
    I hate them all!

Revision.
The dreaded, chilling word
    that haunts school life!
'Revise section one for a test
    on Monday.'
That feared warning that dispels all
    hopes of a weekend's freedom
    and pleasure!

Lord, did you ever have to do an exam?
Did you ever have to revise?
Did you ever sweat over a pile of books,
    counting the days and hours
    to your appointment with the examiner?

Would you be able to cover everything,
    and know all the answers?
Would you pass?

And what if you didn't?
What then, where could you go?
What could you do?

Lord, the questions run round my brain,
    futile and unnecessary,
    as I try to concentrate.
Wondering all the time if I can pass,
    if I have the slightest chance of success.
Will the examiner be kind?
Will they be able to read my writing?
And worst of all, Lord,
    how much time is there left?
The sacrifices have been made,
    free moments become rare pleasures.
Four hours every night,
    shut away with books,
    writing notes,
    and trying to remember
    without cracking under the strain.
With the thought that the future might
    rest on every moment spent revising,
    and wondering why everyone else
    seems to achieve more than me.

Is life a big exam, Lord?
Is each day in itself another test?

With the results written in a large
    record book?
The final mark being read out as you
    approach the Pearly Gates.
And what if you fail?

Am I failing, Lord?
I often wonder.
If it is anything like the rest of my exams
    then I don't stand much chance.

Help me, Lord, to be able to
    pass the test,
    to run life's race,
    and never give up.
To do my best – for you.
And, when swamped by a pile of books,
    and confused by countless questions,
    then help me to pause
    and to give thanks
    that in all the stress,
    the work and the pain,
    I have, at least, the opportunity
    to try to do well.
Thank you, Lord, for that.

Amen.

## MONEY AND POVERTY

Lord, I've just been watching TV.
A millionaire's mansion flashed
    up on the screen,
    complete with private swimming pool,
    tennis courts,
    limousines,
    and security guards.
All that money.
Is it morally right, Lord?
For one person to have so much
    while others have so little?

Believe me, Lord, if I'd worked hard,
    and made myself a million,
    I'd want to keep what I'd earned!
But is that wrong?

Then, Lord, I see other pictures.
I see homeless people on the streets.
I see the tired faces of children living
    in run-down, high-rise flats.
I see the queue of people outside
    the job centre.

The picture changes again,
    as I see another queue, only now they
    stand in line waiting for food.

Queueing in hope
    outside an empty shop – the harvest
    has failed for yet another year.

And as their faces fade from view,
    so others come into focus.
I see a desert,
    some threadbare tents,
    and the occupants dying like flies,
    adult and child alike.
Malnutrition, disease, neglect.

The pictures fade,
    and the last thing I see is a child
    with its tiny hand stretched out
    towards me.
Its eyes are covered with flies,
    its impoverished naked body,
    thin and sickly.
In its eyes I see the hurt of all
    who suffer.
'Why?' it whispers, as the picture dims,
    'Why me?'

So I'm brought back to my own
    selfishness,
    my own thoughtless greed.

I realise how lucky I am
    to be where I am.
To have money,
    to have food and clothing,
    to have the opportunity to
    enjoy my future,
    (to even have a future!)
To have the chance to work, and to live.

Lord, please help me.
Help me to realise how fortunate
    I really am.
Help me to make the most
    of my opportunities
    and to stop being ungrateful.
And at the same time
    never let me forget those
    who have so little;
    the poor and the hungry,
    the homeless and unemployed.
And though I may not be able to
    do much to help them, Lord,
    may I do what I can,
    and always remember them in prayer,
    so that they will know that we both care!

Amen.

# MUSIC

Lord! Hi!
I was just wondering . . .
What's your favourite music?
You see, it just hit me today,
    what a world it'd be without music.
(Where would teenagers be then??!!)
There's so many types,
    so many sounds.
But it's not just sound,
    it's mood,
    thought,
    feeling . . .
An expression of everything, condensed
    into the glory of melody.

Sometimes it makes me want to dance
    (although I'm not much
    good at it, Lord!)
Other times it fills me with happiness,
    and then in a different mood it
    makes me feel sad.
It can pick me up when I'm down,
    or make me stop and think.

But there's other music too, Lord;
    the music around us –
    the sounds of the earth.

(It's as if the world is one large
    concert hall!)

The beautiful song of the bird call,
    the a cappella of the Morning Chorus,
    the deep bass of the frog's throaty song,
    the unending laughter of the
    bubbling beck,
    the steady beat of the rain,
    the soft rustle of the trees . . .

Lord, there's so much music!
So many sounds and so many players,
    be it bird or band,
    record deck or river.
I thank you for them all.
And, Lord, thanks for letting me
    be one of the musicians!

Amen.

## ME

Hi, Lord! It's ME!
Yes, little old me!!
You know, I've never really thought
    about it before,
      but I'd like to say thank you for –
      ME!

I guess I'm usually so lost in my own
    self-pity that I forget.
I forget to look at myself,
    and stop moaning.
If I'd only realise what I've got.
What I am.

So, I'd like to thank you, Lord, for ME!
I know I'm far from perfect,
    but I've still got so much
    to thank you for.
From my little toe on my left foot,
    to my belly-button!
From my sense of humour
    to my smile!
All of it is me,
    your creation, a 'one-off',
    a 'never to be repeated' design,
    a secret mix of ingredients to make a
    totally unique individual.

And that makes me pretty special!
Well, it must mustn't it?
You see, what I'm trying to say
    is that every part of me,
    biological and psychological,
    is from you.
Your gift to me!
Be it my right arm,
    or my sense of smell
It all adds up to ME!
And being that special, makes me
    feel kind of SPECIAL!!
No one else like me;
    unique
    little old me,
    a one off, by God!
What a thought!

So, Lord, again, all I want to
    say is thank you.
Thank you for ME!

Amen.

# DRUGS

Drugs! Why?
Why do people take them?
(Can we talk about it, Lord?)
I just can't understand it.
Why do they do it?
They know it destroys them,
    yet still they crave that 'high'.
So many lives wasted,
    thrown away,
    all because of an exciting kick
    that became an agonising addiction,
    a life of imprisonment.
A sentence of death. Why, Lord?
Why do you allow it?
Can't you stop it?
Is it out of your control?
Is there no cure?

But it's not the drug that's the
    real problem, is it, Lord?
There's more to it than that,
    more than can be seen on the surface.
For there's another problem,
    one that's harder to find,
    harder to come to terms with.
The problem is 'us', Lord.
Humanity in all its greatness,

its striving for power,
for a better life,
a more advanced technology,
has forgotten the little people.
The people who couldn't keep up,
couldn't run the race,
and got left behind.
And instead of waiting, Lord,
humanity just kept on going,
leaving them in its wake;
the unwanted,
the poor,
the homeless,
the hungry,
the drug addict.
For them this was a final grasp
at happiness;
drugs became 'the friend',
always there,
easy to reach,
easy to enjoy.
At last – happiness in a needle.

And they forgot about the pain,
the addiction,
the disease,
DEATH!

Lord, help me,
 for confronted
 with such a problem
 I feel lost and inadequate.
I don't even know how to pray about it.
For what is the solution?
Is there a cure?
I want to see the problem solved,
 I want to find an answer,
 but I don't even know what to ask for.
How can I fight the war on drugs?

Let's be honest, Lord, I can't.
But in all my helplessness,
 I can still pray,
 and feel the need to pray,
 in the hope that, though small,
 it may help.
Lord, please, hear this, my prayer.

Amen.

# HURTING INSIDE

Lord, are you there?
I feel I'm dying inside.
On the outside I'm fine,
    everything's cheery,
    not a care in the world.
But inside, Lord, oh, that's different.
A lot different!
Where has all the laughter gone?
The joy,
    the happiness of the life I
    used to know?
Has it completely gone, Lord,
    out of reach?
For I need it, Lord,
    that fire which burned so strong,
    that now only smoulders,
    burning embers of a distant memory,
    disappearing on the lonely wisp
    of dusty smoke.

Lord, are you listening?
I'm really beginning to wonder.
What is it all about?

I've changed so much, Lord.
But I'm hurting.
My heart is beginning to feel the strain.

Are you wanting this to happen, Lord?
Is it part of your 'Great Plan'?
My faith used to be so strong.
I lived for you,
    loved you.
Yet now . . ?

Now I'm drifting.
I'm confused, unstable,
    with nothing to hold on to.
I have a friend, Lord.
The greatest gift you ever gave.
Someone I trust, and care for
    like no other.
But am I loosing him too?
I'm not angry, Lord,
    he needed what has been given.
But I'm jealous.
Not of him, Lord,
    not of you.
Just jealous.
He is so happy,
    yet the happiness he has is
    still out of my reach.

So again I'm feeling alone.
It's so easy to say,
   'With you I'll never be alone'.
But I'm only human.
How much am I meant to take
   before breaking?
I'm fighting, Lord, but I can't win.
Much more, and I don't think
   I'll get up again.
Can't you see that, Lord?
Hasn't there been enough heartbreak?
Isn't it about time you picked me up,
   out of this choking dust?

Please . . ?

Amen.

# LIFE

Hi, Lord, can we talk?
Just a little 'thank you'.
My life, I'm loving it.
(Well, at the moment anyway!)
It's great.
There's so much to do,
    so many things to see.
It's so exciting.

I know there are hard times.
Times I feel like giving up,
    jacking it all in.
Times when it seems the
    world's against me,
    and everything's going wrong.
But if I just sit back,
    then I see that things aren't
    so bad after all.
It's all had a purpose,
    helped me to grow up in some small way.
And it even seems that there's a
    direction to it all.

Are you guiding me, Lord?
Only it doesn't seem very obvious.
Is there a path you want me to follow?
Is there a way I should take?
(Could I have a map, Lord?)

It's like being on a big expedition,
    the greatest adventure ever.
Round every corner there are
    new things to discover,
    new places to see,
    new people to meet,
    new things to do.
And like every expedition,
    you need to be prepared,
    have the right equipment to survive.
And you've even thought that
    through, Lord.

The most obvious need is a map,
    or a guidebook,
    and what more could we ask for
    – the Bible,
    THE Guide Book!
Every page answers questions,
    poses problems,
    makes me think,
    shows me the Way.

And for any expedition,
    you also need a Guide,
    someone to interpret,
    to help you understand the Map,
    someone who knows the Way,

a person who's been there –
you, Lord,
the best guide in the world!

And that's it.
What an adventure!
You and the Guide Book
    to show us the way!

LET'S GO!

Amen.

## AM I A CHRISTIAN?

Lord, can we talk?
It's about my faith,
    my belief.
You see, as a Christian
    I'm supposed to 'spread the Word',
    'tell the Good News',
    'bring people to Christ'.

To be honest, Lord, I don't,
    (well at least, not very well).
I'm nervous, scared, embarrassed.
'What will people think?'
'I can't tell them, they'll laugh at me.'

It's quite a problem because
    for some reason people ask,
    'Are you a Christian?'
'YES!' I proclaim out loud!
But then they ask, 'Why?'
And that finishes me,
    I'm done for,
    trapped,
    a stuttering mass of confusion,
    lost for words,
    and unable to answer.
    Huh! Some Christian!

I do know why I believe.
(Honest!)
It's just explaining it that's the problem.
Can you give me some help, Lord?
How about a job description,
    guidelines for nervous Christians,
    things to do,
    and not to do,
    when confronted by that 'why?'

I really wish I could hold my ground,
    answer their every question,
    speak your truth,
    proclaim your Word.
Aren't I good enough?
Am I a bad design?
A faulty product?
What am I doing wrong?

Lord, (are you still there?),
    could you give me a hand, please.
I do find it hard to speak out.
So help me when someone asks,
    'Are you a Christian?'
Because maybe if they're asking,
    their reason for doing so

might be me,
my life,
and the way I live it with you.
So who knows, Lord,
maybe I'm getting there after all!

Amen.

# ANOTHER DAY OVER

Well, Lord, that's another day over.
Can we talk?
I've a few things on my mind,
    a few things I need to say.

First, I'm sorry,
    for as with every other day,
    today I've done some things wrong.
In fact, I've done a lot of things wrong,
    and sadly,
    most of the time,
    I'm not even aware of it.
Lord, I hope I haven't hurt anyone,
    or caused too much trouble.
I guess I'll find out tomorrow.
Help me to accept criticism,
    judgement, punishment,
    and help me to learn from my mistakes.

I'd also like to say 'thanks', Lord.
I've quite enjoyed today.
It's good just to be alive,
    seeing friends,
    being outside,
    laughing;
    thanks, Lord.

And then, can I pray for others too, Lord.
It's just that I saw a few friends today
    who need help.
Could you give them a hand,
    help them get sorted out
    and make sense of things?

And finally, can you help me make
    tomorrow a bit better than today?
I don't want to keep messing things up.
Could you give me a hand as well, Lord?

Goodnight.

Amen.

## HAVE ANOTHER

Lord, can we have a chat?
It's about alcohol.
    Beer,
    wine,
    scotch,
    gin,
    and all the rest of it.
Alcohol.

Why do I drink too much of it?
Every time, I say to myself,
    'No more.
    Don't get drunk'.
But I do.
My head starts swimming,
    I find it hard to stand,
    and suddenly everyone else is
    laughing at me.

OK, I'll be honest
    it can be fun,
    'a good sensation'.
But it's still scary,
    not being in total control.
And then, there's always tomorrow!
The headache,
    the nausea,

the sickness,
and the 'wish I was dead' feeling!
And so I say to myself,
    'Never again',
    only to forget it
    the next time round.

Lord, help me to resist,
    to say, 'No',
    to go against the crowd,
    and not just do what they do.

Lord, let my next drink be enjoyable,
    not stupid.

Amen.

# LIKE A THIEF IN THE NIGHT

Lord, can we talk?
I'm a bit scared,
In fact, I'm very scared
It's the 'Second Coming' that's on
    my mind,
      your return to earth.
I find it frightening,
    that you could come at any time,
    even now while I'm praying.
'Like a thief in the night',
    the Bible says.
We don't even know when,
    or where,
    or how.

How will it happen, Lord?
The 'thief in the night' thing gives me
    the impression  it will be quick
    and quiet, and very sudden.
Will you just take Christians?
Will they just disappear?
And what about the rest?
Those you don't take.
Will you give them another chance?
Or is that it?
All over.
The gates of heaven finally locked?

Lord, why can't you just appear?
Now.
Prove you are who you say you are.
Wouldn't it be easier?
You'd have the world at your feet.
But, Lord, who am I to question
    your plans?

Lord, I am frightened.
You see, I don't think I'm good enough
    and I'm afraid you'll leave me behind.
Help me to be ready,
    to be prepared.
Because when you come again
    I don't think I'll have a second chance.

Amen.

# FEELING DOWN

Lord, I've got to talk.
You got a minute?
It's just that I'm feeling down,
    and I don't know why.
Why am I unhappy?
I've great friends, parents,
    music, you, life.
What could be wrong?
I don't know, I just feel down.
I'm sick of being taken for granted
    and ignored.
'Oh, Dave doesn't mind.'
'Dave's OK, he'll listen.'
'He's a good laugh, is Dave.'
I'm not OK!
Why don't people realise?
I'm waiting for someone to come along
    and look a little deeper.
To peel away the make-up and look at
    the real me.
I'm lonely, Lord, so lonely.
Yes, I've friends, but it's a different kind
    of loneliness.
The kind that haunts you in a crowd
    jumps on you when you're
    with a friend.
Stabs you in the back

when you're by yourself.
So many times I've wanted to scream,
   and reach out for someone.
Someone to hold,
   someone with the loving
   support I need so much.
That tiny bit of affection,
   a genuine love that asks nothing
   more of me than what I have.
Yet, when I reach out
   it's gone.
A shadow in the darkness.
Why is it, Lord?
I'm sorry, but I can't understand.
WHY ME? What have I done?
Why can't I show my inner self?
That part of me so few have seen.
The quiet, understanding me,
   the caring, loving me,
   the happy, warm me.
What am I doing wrong?
Does anyone understand?
I'm feeling alone again, Lord.
Left alone in the dark as my
   friends move on.
Why won't they look over
   their shoulders?

See me kneeling in the dust, crying, hurt?
Don't they realise, Lord?
I want to cry, but I can't.
What do I do?
Shout for them to stop?
Help me, Lord.
I'm so frightened, lost, alone.
Help me, Lord.
I love you,
    but does anyone really love me?

'My child,
    don't you remember
    my footsteps in the sand?
When there was only one set
    you asked me why I had left you?
Can't you remember, my child,
    I then carried you!
My love for you is unending,
    so do not worry.
Lean on my love and trust me.
I will carry you
    when you grow weary.'

Amen.

# DEATH

Lord, you got a minute?
It's just that I'm a bit bothered,
    about death.
Such a horrible word.
The dreaded cloaked skeleton,
    carrying his scythe.
But why is it such a fearful thing?
Everyone dies, sooner or later,
    so what's the problem?
Well, with me, Lord,
    it's because it is certain.
That for me is frightening.
No matter what happens
    one thing's for sure:
    I will die.
Just the thought
    raises all manner of questions.
How will I die?
    Will it be painful?
    When will it happen?
    What will be the cause?
    What happens once I'm dead?

You see, God,
    two lads I've known,
    both my age,
    have died this year.

One killed in a motor bike accident,
    the other died of asthma.
And that really brought it home.
They no longer exist on this earth.
They're gone.
Just memories.
It really made me think.
Are they with you now, Lord?
Do you hold them close?

Lord, this heaven and hell business
    is so hard to understand.
I have so many friends I love
    that I know aren't Christians.
Will you condemn them?
Will you, lover of each
    and every one of us,
        condemn those who don't believe?
Don't you think that's a bit off?
Evil in fact?
Unjust?
And how, Lord, are you going
    to distinguish me from them?
OK, Lord, I believe in you,
    and I do my best to follow you.
But I can be disgusting,
    a bad example of Christianity.

Doing things that are wrong,
    'sinning without thinking'.
Why do you love me, Lord?
I've sometimes wondered if you do.
Will I die only to be cast into hell?
Does anyone really deserve that?
Do they, Lord?

'David, of course I love you,
    I love everyone.
If you only knew how much!
If one is lost, my heart bleeds.
If one is saved, all of heaven rejoices!
Let me worry about everyone else.
I'm just saying to you,
    'Follow me'.

Amen.

# DISCRIMINATION

Lord, can we talk?
Something's bothering me.
It's beginning to make me feel a bit upset.
What do people think of me, Lord?
Do they really like me?
You see I heard something today.
Something someone had said about me.
It wasn't really all that nice, Lord.
It was from a friend.

Why do people do that?
Why be two-faced?
Just because I was a bit different.
Mind you, I guess everyone's guilty.
Judging only on the little I see.
If someone is serious,
    then they are depressing.
If someone is happy and full of jokes,
    then they love themselves.
If someone is proud of something they've done,
    then they are big-headed.

See what I mean, Lord?
People jump to conclusions.
Just because of the way someone is
    different to you.
Then you don't like them.

It's not just small things either.
Colour,
    race,
    sex,
    belief
    age.
All make people different.
All cause problems.

I must admit, Lord, that being white
    I don't really know what it's like to
    be on the receiving end of racism.
To be singled out because you're black.
To be hated because of your colour.
So wrong, Lord, so wrong.
So why does it happen?
It's like a disease.
Discrimination.
Labelled because you're different.
No one is left untouched.
It spreads through society.
Every age,
    sex,
    colour,
    race.

Apartheid in South Africa.
Blacks oppressed.
Why?
Because they're black.

Sexism from both sides.
Each thinking they're better than the other.
What happened to Equality?

Anti semitism.
Jews blamed for the downfall of Germany.
A scapegoat.
Genocide.

Ageism.
People aren't employed
    because they're too old.
All youngsters are vandals.

And the list goes on, Lord.
Sad really.
So much hate.
So little reason.

Lord, it's such a huge problem.
I feel out of my depth thinking about it.
Help me not to discriminate.
Just because someone is different.
Help me to realise we are all equal.

All human.
All loved.
By you.

Amen.